I Can Read About
Planets

Written by Darrow Schecter
Illustrated by Tom LaPadula

Troll Associates

This edition published in 2003.

Illustrations copyright © 1996 by Tom LaPadula.

Text copyright © 1996 by Troll Communications L. L. C.

Published by Troll Associates, an imprint and registered trademark of Troll Communications L. L. C.

Printed in the United States of America.

10 9 8

Library of Congress Cataloging-in-Publication Data
Schecter, Darrow.
    I can read about planets / by Darrow Schecter ; illustrated by
Tom LaPadula.
    p. cm.
  ISBN 0-8167-3636-7 (lib. bdg.) — ISBN 0-8167-3637-5 (pb.)
  1. Planets—Juvenile literature.   [1. Planets.]   I. LaPadula,
Tom, ill.   II. Title.
  QB602.S34   1996
  523.4—dc20   95-5948

The word planet means *wanderer*. The ancient Greeks called the planets wanderers because the planets changed their positions in the sky.

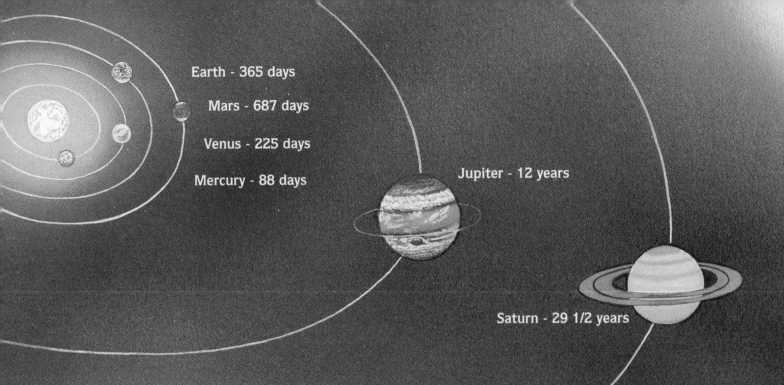

Earth - 365 days

Mars - 687 days

Venus - 225 days

Mercury - 88 days

Jupiter - 12 years

Saturn - 29 1/2 years

Today we know that each planet moves around the sun. The journey that each planet makes around the sun is called an *orbit*.

Each planet is found at a different distance from the sun.
This is why it takes each planet a different length
of time to orbit the sun.

Pluto - 248 years

Uranus - 84 years

Neptune - 165 years

What exactly is a planet? Planets are sometimes called heavenly bodies. This means that they are found in space. Scientists who study the planets and other things in space are called astronomers. They often do their work in an observatory. They study the planets with high-powered telescopes, computers, and space satellites.

Ranger 7

Moon

Earth

Astronomers have discovered many things about the planets and stars. All stars are really suns. Some stars are very much like our own sun. Our sun is much larger than any of the planets.

Stars give off their own light. But planets do not give off their own light. They are like mirrors. They reflect light the way our moon reflects light from the sun.

The planets seem to move very fast. But this is only because the planets are closer to us than stars. Stars are much, much farther away.

All planets orbit the sun. Some planets have smaller bodies that also orbit around them. These bodies are called moons or natural satellites.

Moons and satellites travel close to the planet they are orbiting. Their journey around the planet is always a shorter trip than the planet's journey around the sun.

The sun and the nine planets that orbit it make up most of our solar system.

The first four planets are called the inner planets.

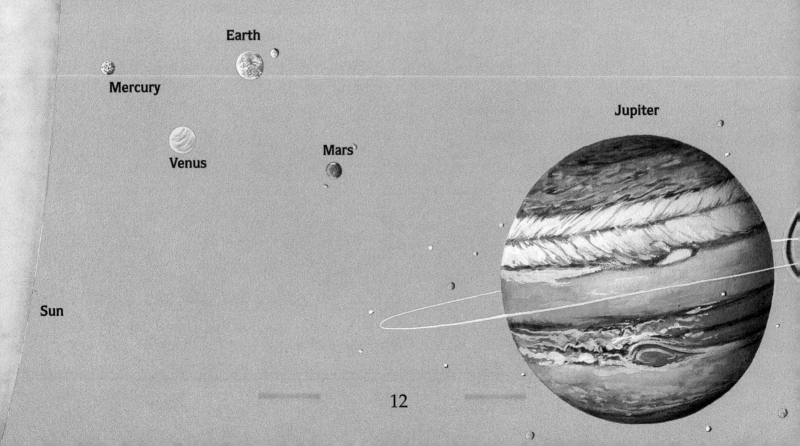

Earth

Mercury

Venus

Mars

Jupiter

Sun

The last five are called the outer planets.

The planet closest to the sun is called Mercury. It is one of the smallest planets in our solar system. It is 36 million miles (58 million kilometers) away from the sun.

There are things about Mercury you would probably like and things you would not like. It takes Mercury only 88 days to orbit the sun. This means that a year on Mercury is only 88 days. If you lived on Mercury, your birthday would come four times as often as on Earth.

But since this planet is so close to the sun, Mercury may become as hot as 648 degrees Fahrenheit (342 degrees Celsius) on its surface.

The planet after Mercury is Venus. Venus is like Earth in many ways. Astronomers call Venus the twin sister of Earth.

Venus is 67 million miles (108 million kilometers) from the sun. A year on Venus is 225 days long. It takes Venus longer to go around the sun than it takes Mercury. Venus is famous because it is brighter than any of the other planets. Only the sun and the moon are brighter in the sky than Venus.

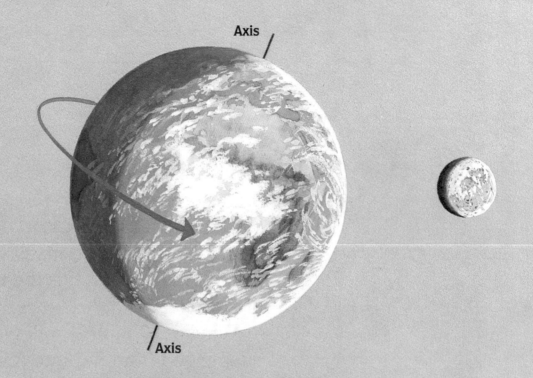

Axis

Axis

You already know about the third planet from the sun because you live on it. Our planet Earth is the third planet. It is 93 million miles (150 million kilometers) away from the sun. Earth has a natural satellite—the moon.

As Earth orbits the sun, it is also spinning like a top. Earth is rotating on an imaginary line through its center. This line is called Earth's axis. In 24 hours, Earth spins completely around.

When our side of Earth turns toward the sun, we have day. When our side of Earth turns away from the sun, we have night.

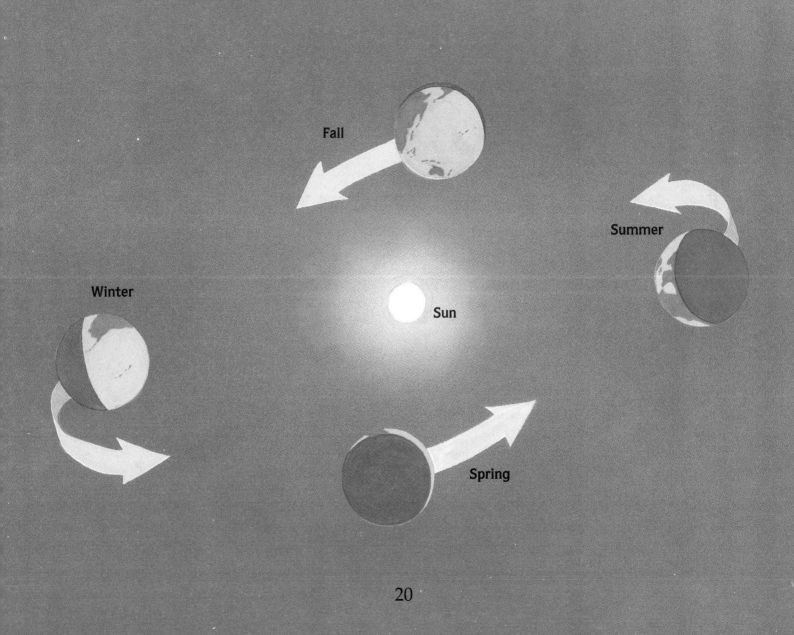

Fall

Summer

Winter

Sun

Spring

Earth tilts as it orbits the sun, shifting its position in relation to the sun. As a result, different parts of Earth get different amounts of sunlight during Earth's 365-day trip around the sun. This causes the seasons.

Why does it get cold in winter? During the winter, our part of Earth is tilted away from the sun and gets less of the sun's rays. During the summer, our part of Earth is tilted toward the sun and gets more direct sunlight.

Earth's tilting also causes the in-between seasons of spring and fall. It helps the flowers to blossom in spring and the leaves to fall in autumn. Winter, spring, summer, and fall: Our tilting Earth travels around the sun in a year's journey.

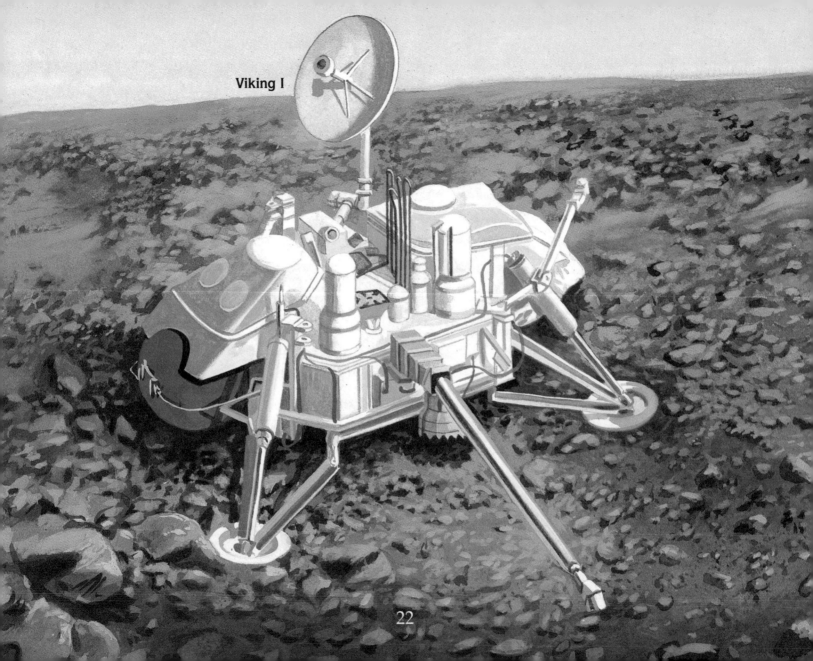

Viking I

Mars is the fourth planet. It is 142 million miles (228 million kilometers) from the sun. Mars is named after the Roman god of war because of its red, warlike color. Mars has seasons because it tilts toward the sun the way Earth tilts toward the sun.

Spacecraft have studied the soil of Mars and have sent back photographs of the surface of Mars.

It takes Mars 687 days to orbit the sun. Every 15 to 17 years, Mars comes very close to Earth and the sun. This is a good time for scientists on Earth to study Mars.

There are two satellites around Mars. Their names are Deimos and Phobos.

Deimos

Phobos

Sun

Earth

The fifth planet is
Jupiter, the largest of all known planets. It is
483 million miles (778 million kilometers) from the
sun. This planet is eleven times larger in diameter than
Earth. Jupiter is one of the brightest planets. It has bands of
different colors across it. Jupiter also has a large reddish spot.

Jupiter

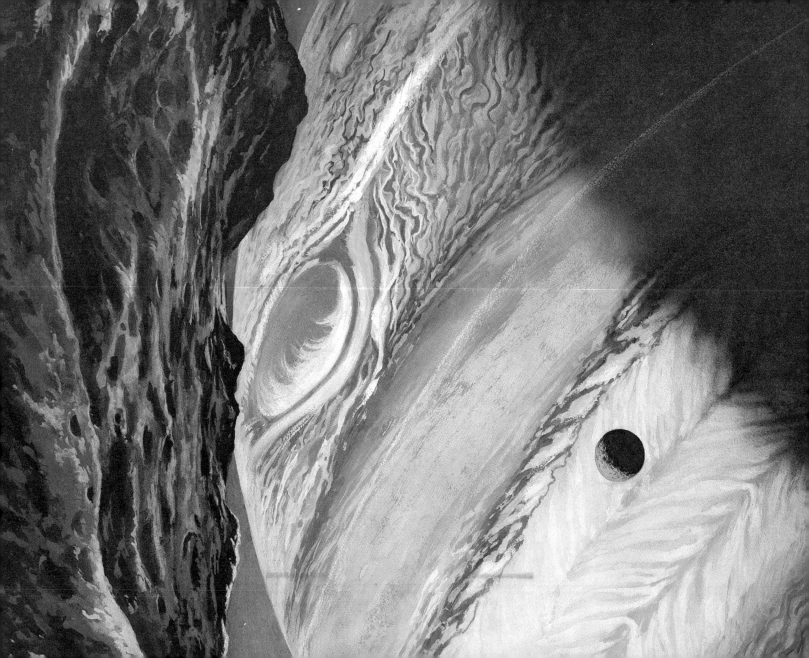

Jupiter is puzzling to astronomers because its actual surface cannot be seen through a telescope. It is hidden by clouds of swirling gases.

Jupiter is 483 million miles (778 million kilometers) from the sun. If you're on Jupiter, you'll have to wait 12 years to complete one orbit around the sun.

Saturn is the sixth planet. It is the second largest planet. Only Jupiter is larger. Saturn is 889 million miles (1,430,000,000 kilometers) from the sun.

Saturn is famous
for its rings. At one time
astronomers thought that
there was only one ring.
Later they discovered that
there were many icy rings
around Saturn.

Saturn is the farthest planet from the sun that you can see without a telescope. Bring your warmest clothes if you ever visit Saturn. Its average temperature is 285 degrees below zero Fahrenheit (141 degrees below zero Celsius). Saturn has at least 23 satellites. The largest is named Titan, but you need a telescope to see it. Some of Saturn's moons are so small they cannot be seen from Earth at all. Using the Hubble Space Telescope, scientists have found at least two new moons close to Saturn's surface.

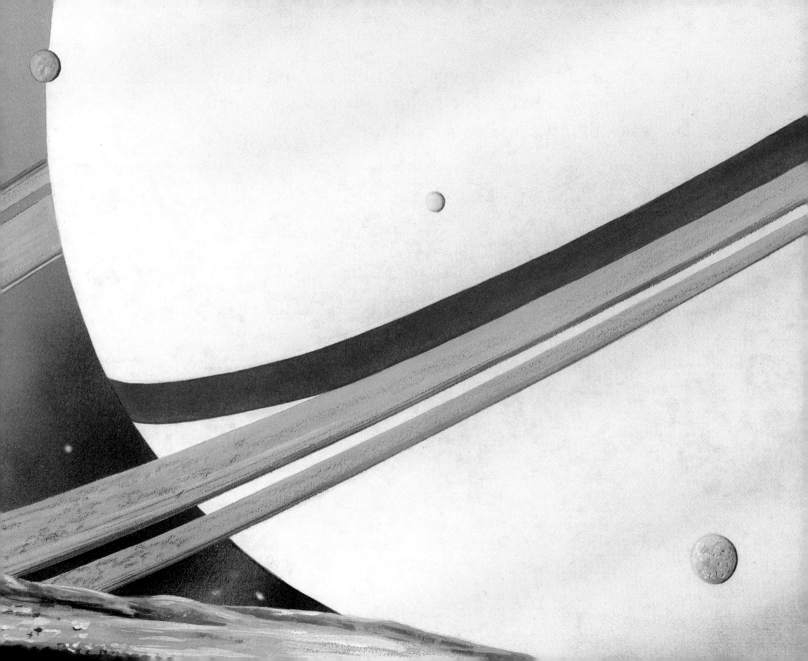

The last three planets are very far from the sun. They are so far away that no one can be exactly sure what they are really like. There is still much to learn about them.

Pluto

Neptune

Uranus

The seventh planet is called Uranus. It is 1,790,000,000 miles (2,880,000,000 kilometers) from the sun. When viewing Uranus through a telescope, astronomers can see a faint green glow. Uranus has 15 moons and at least nine rings around it. Since Uranus is so far away, it takes this planet 84 years to orbit the sun.

Uranus

Neptune is the eighth planet from the sun. For many years Neptune was thought to be the farthest planet from the sun, until the discovery of Pluto! Neptune is extremely far—2,800,000,000 miles (4,500,000,000 kilometers)—from the sun and very, very cold. Every 165 years Neptune completes its orbit around the sun.

And finally there is the ninth planet, Pluto. Pluto is the farthest planet from the sun that we know of. It is more than 3½ billion miles (5½ billion kilometers) from the sun. Pluto has one moon named Charon.

Pluto is a tiny planet that was discovered by astronomers in 1930. It is so small that astronomers used to believe that Pluto was not a planet, but a moon that had left Neptune's orbit. Because it is so far away, Pluto is still a very mysterious planet.

We cannot be
certain what lies beyond
the edges of our solar system,
but new discoveries are always
being made. Using the Hubble Space
Telescope, scientists confirmed that there
is a ring made up of millions of comets
surrounding our solar system.

Our solar system is part of the universe. And the universe is a never-ending wonder that has puzzled and amazed people since the beginning of time. Someday, with the help of telescopes that scientists have sent into space, we may discover new planets.

Hubble Space Telescope

And, in time to come, we will learn more about the mysteries of outer space.

INDEX